Test Paper

Linda Cash

Templar Poetry

First Published 2007 by Templar Poetry
Templar Poetry is an imprint of Delamide and Bell

Fenelon House,
Kingsbridge Terrace
Dale Road, Matlock, Derbyshire
DE4 3NB

www.templarpoetry.co.uk

ISBN 978-1-906285-02-9

Copyright © Linda Cash 2007

Author has asserted her right to be identified
as the author of this work in accordance
with the Copyright, Designs and Patents Act 1988.

All rights reserved. This book is sold subject to the condition
that it shall not, by way of trade or otherwise, be lent, resold, hired out
or otherwise circulated without the publisher's prior consent, in any form
of binding or cover other than that in which it is published and without
a similar condition including this condition being imposed on
the subsequent purchaser.

For permission to reprint or broadcast these poems write to
Templar Poetry

Typeset by Pliny
Graphics by Paloma Violet
Printed and bound in India

For Rosie and Tim

Acknowledgements

Acknowledgements are due to the editors of the following publications, where some of these poems were first published: Smiths Knoll (*Aromatherapy Kit*, 2005), Acumen (*Woman with Exploding Head*, 2006), and Iota (*On Chicken and Forgiveness*, 2005 & *The Orchid Prison*, 2007).

Thanks to Tim Zekki for his encouragement and understanding when I'm 'somewhere else' writing, and my daughter for her enthusiasm and support - and lack of teenage embarrassment about her mother writing poetry.

I'd like to thank my virtual writing friends: Nell Grey, Joan Ryder, Allison McVety, Helen Hudspith, James Graham, and Julie Balloo. They made me do it.

Contents

Compulsion 1 - 1
Compulsion 2 - 3
Aromatherapy Kit - 4
On Chicken and Forgiveness - 6
The Orchid Prison - 8
Woman with Exploding Head - 10
Tell Me Exactly What Happened - 11
Lake Echo - 13
The Strangers On The Lawn - 14
The Dandelion Clock - 16
As Haddock Is To Milk - 18
Siren - 19
Hotel Des Arts - 20
Punctuation - 21
Half Life Crisis - 23
Capsules - 25
Rush - 27
Medical Notes - 28
Test Paper - 30

Compulsion 1

The colour of his mother's new fangled
cake mixer or his Uncle's Robin Reliant

(and as fragile) it slipped easily into
his anorak pocket and he and his friend

walked calmly out of the building, squinting
into the sunlight, a thousand eyes

following, while it seemed to emanate guilt
through layers of quilted nylon. For years

it lay in his father's old cigar box
like a dirty secret, under the bed

with the magazines he'd found amongst
the sharp smelling leaf mould in the woods

(that smell would always remind him of the first time
he discovered what older boys were talking about)

and later it lay, pushed to the back
of a drawer, in various houses,

in a succession of counties, through two
wives and three children, until he could bear

it no longer - forty-three years on
he returned it, intact, to the museum

with a letter of apology,
and it was carefully placed back in the case,

on top of its faded description:
The Egg of the Little Bustard.

Compulsion 2

Fingers glide across parchment skin, smooth it
with gloved hands, he breathes in deeply the silence,

hushed voices, the clip clop of heels then, slash
slash, slash, (hush, hush), slicing through arterial

rivers he amputates whole continents
with surgical precision. He's been careful

to place himself out of the reach of
CCTV. He's the ripper of

Bloomsbury, the stalker of Holborn;
he bends her, folds her, apologising,

slips her into his calf skin leather case
and standing, zips up. He's done. He keeps her

in a draughtsman's chest between layers
of tissue - acid free, between

Mercator and Speed, but when the knock comes
he's already fed her to the shredder.

Aromatherapy Kit

Imagine being that woman who spent so long
loving someone, nearly a million years, she said.
Or was it ten weeks?

Loving him not for what he was
or what he gave her, for all he ever gave her
was a small white box made of card.

But loving him for what he wasn't,
because he wasn't like other men.
Which was probably why he gave her

that small white box with its ten tiny bottles,
regimented, each waiting be called up to do their bit
in the war against stresses and strains.

Uniform bottles of precious oils in shades of ochre,
deepest honey, pale yellow, and orchid white.
Like a little row of urine samples, she thought, much later.

She'd save them for special occasions, weekends, birthdays
and Christmas, when he couldn't be with her. She'd bathe in
                                                         the oils,
heady from the ylang ylang and vetivert

and a single glass of champagne. Sliding the oils
over her body, tracing his movements,
remembering him with the tips of her fingers

she'd call him on his mobile, making him moan
in the cold spare room, sitting on a pile of his wife's ironing,
until he'd say he had to go, to put the kids to bed.

She kept each little bottle in its box, even when it was used up.
Each with it's printed name on frosted glass;
Relax, De-stress, Unwind, Rescue, Revive.

Ten magical little bottles, all the same. All empty.

On Chicken and Forgiveness

That day she'd felt a spasm return
distant as the sound of the playground
the feeling of being last to be picked for the team,
or seeing her best friend and the new girl
giggling behind hands.

It rose inside but found nowhere to go,
a blow to the nose transposed to the stomach
it made her want to leave this place
to be beamed up to a parallel universe
where none of it happened
or ever happens.

If only it was as certain
as locking herself in the loo, heart thumping
watching the blue wave wash through
one window and settle in its twin,
sometime relentless
sometime faltering
or the litmus turning pink to blue.
She wants the certainty of chemistry.

How can you possibly tell?
It's not like the dipstick in the oil
(the engine must be cold)
or flinging the pasta against the wall
(if it sticks it's done)
even pulling the leg from the thigh
(there must be no blood).

She needs a sure sign,
like ten centimetres dilated,
like the canary falling off its perch.

How do you know when you've forgiven?
"Your forgiveness has been processed,
please keep this receipt for your records."
Something to file with the decree nisi
and decree absolute.
If only it was as definite as that.

The Orchid Prison

She candles eggs for omens,
checks each lemon for signs,
wraps them in newspaper.

She'd hold a wolf by the ears,
if it would bring him to her.
Every day now there's a story

of the border being re-opened.
Some fight to keep it shut,
the wise keep quiet.

She collects wild orchid honey
the way her father told her,
under a veil. In long white gloves.

If the bees work hard for her
one day she'll have enough money
for a ferry to the mainland.

Does she keep bees, or do they keep her?
They are free to go. Do they ever venture across,
feed on his flowers, buzz past his ear?

At night she flies on the back
of a giant worker bee, its body vibrating,
silky filaments brushing her thighs,

they fly in formation with the swarm,
pausing for orchids, jasmine and almond blossom,
circling Bellapais Abbey in a victory roll,

buzzing Byzantine churches, only ascending
to be out of range of the soldiers
of the UN buffer zone, she holds tight

til the other side of the Troodos mountains.
In the morning she smiles to herself,
Are lovers lunatics?

Woman with Exploding Head

When it happened for the second time that week
she thought she really ought to see someone
but she imagined the imperceptible shift of the doctor's eyebrow

when she explained the nuclear fission in her head
and the suggestion it might be beneficial if she got plugged
into the national grid

Meanwhile fighter planes with improbable names
rev up in her temporal lobes
rivers run, crashing through weirs, slinging canoes against the rocks
and little glittery fishes scatter into the night

the earth splits into a million pieces
yet another big bang and she wakes,
damp, and a little surprised to be alive

Tell me Exactly what Happened

There's blood in your mouth.
Everything is singing in a minor key
in your house of honey and moonshine.

The rushing seas have receded leaving
fragments from the wreck of a previous life.
Your future stretches out flat and shimmering in the heat.

It's my turn to rescue you,
you who were always the shining one,
the one with the grades, the highlights and the houses.

My hair is full of fairies blown across the water.
Maybe they'll take root, send out searching tentacles,
make me Medusa again.

The idiot savant with the burlap sack.
smiles at us with expensive teeth,
says, 'Cheer up it might never happen.'

Outside the wheatgrass café
the man with his life in a shopping trolley
argues the toss with the space in front of him.

(When people hang out with imaginary people
why are they never their friends?)
The street cleaner in the Viking helmet moves him on.

A woman uncertain on high heels totters past, a lollipop
lady's coat over her arm. "My new career," you say.
We look at each other and break into giggles.

You pat your swollen lip, "It beats collagen."
With a bottle of chilled Chablis, and your Burberry Filofax
we plan the next stage of your life.

Ice wrapped in a linen napkin soothes your eye.

Lake Echo

Skimming stones, between the fizz of static,
the radio not quite tuned to the charts,

she smiles like a megaphone while he
unzippers fish, slits gizzards, trims fins.

Solid at the centre of her universe, she's oblivious
to the low hum of the world pivoting round her.

She brings berries, shoots heat-seeking smiles
sticky berry juice on thighs, she wants and wants.

As the trout shimmers and thrashes
on the hook, she reels him in.

The Strangers on the Lawn

If you stare long enough
into a tin of morello cherries
it looks like blood in a tin can,
and you can see the stained raspberry sticks
that grew in your grandmother's garden
and pick up the metallic taste
of flinty soil.

Stare again,
go back further, and remember
how at night there were signals across the water
that stopped
when your mother
came into the room to pull the curtain.
You'd hear her go back down the stairs,
an angel in work boots,
smoothing a marble in her palm.

Remember too,
the strangers on the lawn
always on the lawn,
sometimes with a glass of champagne,
the high tinkle of laughter and glasses,
your mother in her party shoes
that pinched her toes,
though she never stopped smiling.
The last time the strangers came
they wore paper body suits.

The police in the driveway, blue lights
flashing
like the lights over the water,
silently.
A cat's cradle of tape tied from tree to tree
and a golden lozenge against cumulus,
the day your kite broke away.

The Dandelion Clock

She had it all shorn off when she started the chemo,
now it's grown back to half an inch in length,

bleached blonde with a hint of nicotine.
She passes her hand over it, feeling it flip back and forth.

She thinks she looks like a dandelion clock,
but doesn't know how much time she's got. She has

a list of what she must do before she goes.
Giving up the roll-ups is not on the list. Stable and door,

she says with a wink. She wants to be painted naked,
with more honesty than tenderness.

Picasso would've done a good job, she says.
She's busy collecting ex-lovers, thinks it funny

to ask if they own a black tie. She washes down
antioxidants and milk thistle with vodka,

pulls her tee shirt up in bars to show
where they took a piece of flesh from her back,

wears a turquoise frothy bra revealed
by a shirt undone just a button too far.

At least, she thinks, she'll never do beige.

As Haddock is to Milk

As haddock is to milk, to ill in bed,
as chilli is to squid, to vodka shots,
to late nights, to throbbing heads.
As salmon is to blinis,
as chamomile is to sunburned skin,
as arnica is to bruises.

Siren

The nightly urban wave
of police cars has passed.
It's eighty-five

degrees Fahrenheit,
windows yawn
in the stifling heat,

our wooden floor
is littered with cats
flat-out in dead-cat pose.

Like a dream
metallic red cuts through the black,
a scream, streets away,

then nothing.
You shift slightly,
guilty, I still you.

Hotel des Arts

I'm here, in the sigh of the midnight train
pulling out of La Gare Du Nord.

I'm here in South Beach, in the hiss
of unexpected rain on the sidewalk.

You see my shape in the heap of unmade bed,
trace me through the paper chase of the bathroom.

I'm here in the slightest swagger of hips
or a certain look in a porn star's eyes,

I'm hiding in this month's 'Loaded' model's parted lips.
You feel me as the slightest pressure,

and a subliminal rise in temperature on your thighs.
Listen, can you hear a single pearl roll across the floor?

Punctuation

I always had this feeling as a child
that I could just stop, just stop being.

Not stop breathing, more simple than that.
Just stop existing, if I chose.

Of course, older, I tried not to think about it
in case I made the wrong decision,

and became non-existent, and regretted it later.
Though there would be no 'later', I supposed.

But then, I also had this feeling
that there was really was something

inside those tiny gold, red and green foiled packets
hanging on the Christmas tree.

Presents for fairies, I imagined.
I pick out the pine needles caught in my socks, and wait.

Tuck my knees under my chin. And wait.
You don't say a word, because you are afraid.

You're afraid that the words
will burst up through your throat,

jangling through your vocal chords
and escape, to hang in the air, the unsaid finally said.

And they do. They float in the air -
I can almost see the quote marks around them,

the words, "I want, I want to be with her,"
quiver for a moment, and drop.

I watch a gilded angel on the tree
turning in the draught from the chimney.

It has a bow and arrow - I'd never noticed that before.
Since when was cupid part of the nativity scene?

Once you've gone I sweep up
the shattered pieces of glass bauble under the tree.

Half Life Crisis

After you'd gone I turned the key in the lock
and found an unemployed angel
crumpled as a used Kleenex, flaked out
on the sofa in my old dressing gown,
pulling out feathers
and picking at Pringles.

Well, what can you do when
your mind changes you?
Your ego swept in, saying 'all change'
leaving you in the wrong place
with all the wrong people.

I'd continued to give you rock
when suddenly you wanted sand.
I was constant cinnabar
when what you needed
was mercury, or uranium.
I guess it was a half-life crisis.

Hang the phone back on the hook,
put the tears back in your eyes
you can't unbruise the peach,
or make the river run backwards.

I'm not sure carbon is a girl's best friend.
Are stable elements eternal?

The Samaritans were very nice,
but slightly distracted,
they told me I must feel awful.
Well I think I knew that anyway,
and I sensed slight disappointment
when I said I wasn't planning anything silly.

So, the angel and I opened a bottle
and talked about men for hours.
That night we took turns feeding the baby
and vowed to go out clubbing one day.
I knew we never would.

Now all the Cherubims are bulimic,
and they've shaved their heads in cancer chic,
St Peter's lost the plot - the exalted book's
been transcribed to Excel
and crashes as badly as a fallen angel.

Capsules

Light's leaking from a crack under the door
bleaching the reclaimed pine pale.

Atoms and electrons interconnecting
she's no longer sure where he ends, and she begins.

She sleeps with him because it feels so totally right.

In a strange bed, blue light, white thighs, it feels so good
and so bad, he hears himself sigh.

It's raining in a strange city and he has time to kill.

She closes the door leaving voices behind in the dark.
There's a dynamo at the centre of her soul.

She slept with him because he gave away his kidney.

There's safety in chopping avocados. Later
he relinquishes himself to the mopping of blood.

He slept with him because it had been a long time.

There's a pentagram over the toilet and blood
on the ceiling, people in the kitchen she doesn't know.

But it was too late to get a cab.

In his pocket he keeps a jar, he says it contains
a lovers last breath. He dreams of girls with guns.

He slept with her because he can.

She painted the sofa with red gloss paint
it's meant to reflect her loss but it just pisses off the land-
lord.

She slept with him to prove she's still a woman.

His ECG travelled mountains and verdant passes
untill it reached the savanna, nirvana.

He'd slept with her because it seemed right.

Upstairs the gods are playing marbles, there's a crack
in the universe where all the trouble starts.

Meteorites are ripening in the sun.

Rush

Metaphors are mixing in the sky. Is the bird
a metaphor for a plane, or vice versa?
The planes are stiff and unwieldy
descending in regular slots: one minute and ten seconds;
the birds free-wheel in their own holding pattern.

I've spent the whole day archiving my dreams
after reading a self-help book. I think I misread something.
You tell me there's as much bad poetry
as bad porn on the Internet. I wonder
which would destroy the soul first in a double-blind

clinical trial. You sit and nod in agreement
at the ads on the TV. Quick. We haven't much time,
the end of the world is nigh, assemble the props:
you'll need your drug of choice,
a box of toys, and your favourite fantasy.

Together we watch the faces pass
the sheer glass expanse of our 25th floor apartment.
I'm still not sure if this is the rapture,
or even which way up I am.

Medical Notes

So, I went for an x-ray of my soul. And I saw it there,
right on the screen, a delicate arc of deepest crimson,
but the darkest part, obsidian, leaching into purple,

like blotting paper. There were notes and memos
etched across it, forgotten loves, old pain, all so
saturated by ink or tears it was pulling itself apart.

It was in danger of collapsing, the consultant said.
He thought that probably the blue areas were caused
by reports read in the papers, lilac tones

for when the phone rang late at night. He asked
if I'd ever worked in the City and he winced
when I told him about the job in the call centre.

Now, he said, it's time to have a think
because it might be best to part with it now,
as it's perfectly possible to have a normal life

without a soul at all. Then he name-dropped
a few celebs he'd had under his scalpel.
He said they were tricky buggers, souls,

but he'd whip it out under local anaesthetic.
I'd be right as rain. Just a little bruised and delicate
for a week or two. I'd be able to do anything as usual,

apart from writing and painting. And I should avoid
ballet, opera, and poetry as it was possible I'd have
an adverse reaction. But I could read the tabloid papers,

and magazines such as Heat and Hello. He warned
me off sunsets, and newborn babies' smiles, apparently
it could cause untold damage as my system

adjusted. I said I'd think about it, stuffed the papers
into my pocket, and emerged dazed into the sunlit car park.
Apart from the odd twinge, it wasn't exactly chronic.

I decided I'd check out alternative therapies, turn off reality TV,
and keep my soul. Then I heard on the news about the illegal
second-hand soul trade, and the Internet spare parts market.

It was possible mine was earmarked for ebay -
if your doctor wants to remove your soul, be warned.

Test paper

1. a. Why does the woman wake screaming every night?
   b. What does this tell us about her state of mind?

2. What song does she hear in the wires?

3. What is the significance of the walnut box?

4. What premonitions would you expect her to see?

5. What does she see in the peeled-back sides of the demolished houses?

6. In this sense, what is the meaning of a pathetic fallacy?

7. Who 'cries like an icebox left open all night?'

8. What does the child represent?

9. What is the symbolism of the vodka jello?

10. Discuss the similiarities between spilt milk and a tungsten light bulb.

11. What did the woman keep in an old Strepsils tin?

12. Why are Strepsils 'curiously strong?'

13. Who had 'a sneeze like a bomb exploding in a suitcase?'

14. At the end, why does the old man throw his Wellingtons on the fire?

15. Where does Icarus come into all this?

16. In what ways does history repeat itself?

17. What is the writer trying to say?

18. Explore the various parallels drawn between desire and death, love and war.

19. 'A lop-sided smile, a metal plate in the hip, and a scar that jaggered and stuttered across his chest.' What else appealed to her about him?

20. Why did she say that her bones were full of sky, her legs as weak as a newborn pelican, but her eyes as sharp as the knives in ex-lover's minds?

21. Why did she describe him as 'cold and empty as a disused hospital?'

22. Do you think she was inconsistent?

23. Would you describe him as brooding and enigmatic? Or just a bit of a prat?

24. Do you think men are all the same?

25. Do you realise how beautiful you look without those glasses?